My Animal
Counting
Book

Illustrated by RENE CLOKE

1 dog

2 cats

3 pigs

4
squirrels

5 turtles

6
birds

7 foxes

8 mice

9
lambs

10 ducks

11

butterflies

12

rabbits

4 turtles

2 lettuces

6 rabbits

7 carrots

2 dogs

1 bone

11 mice

8 cookies

15 hens

10 chicks

1 pig

12 acorns

3 donkeys

3 saddles

9 frogs

4 lilies

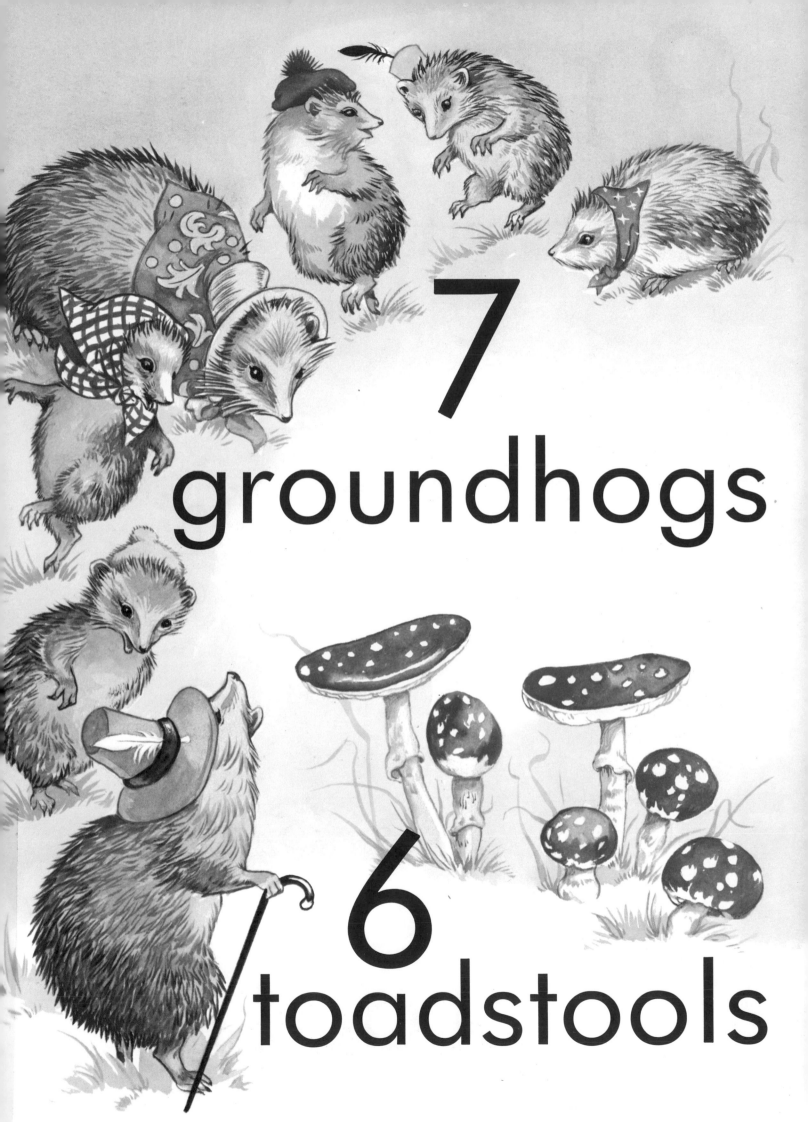

7 groundhogs

6 toadstools

10 hamsters

12 grapes

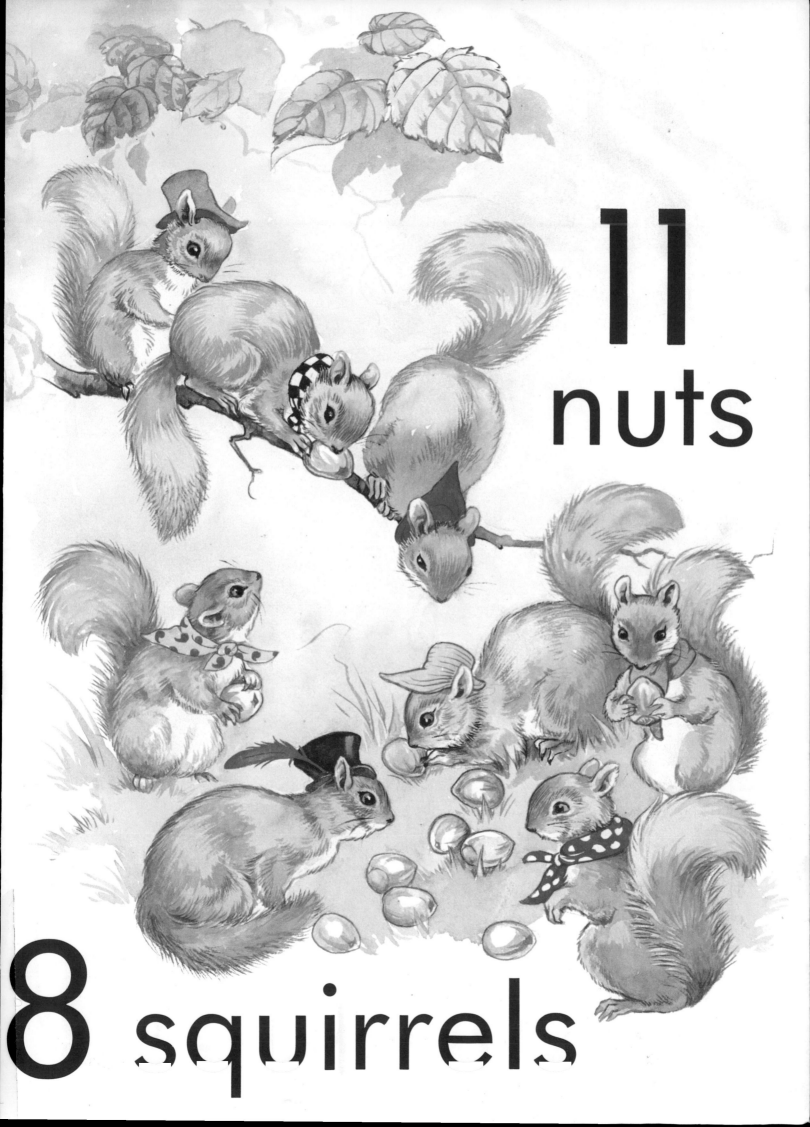

11 nuts

8 squirrels